To Ted
Every Blessing
Zeph 3:17

POWER FROM ON HIGH

30 · 1 · 08

Martin Tuson

authorHOUSE®

AuthorHouse™ UK Ltd.
500 Avebury Boulevard
Central Milton Keynes, MK9 2BE
www.authorhouse.co.uk
Phone: 08001974150

First published by AuthorHouse 12/11/2007

ISBN: 978-1-4343-5317-7 (sc)

Printed in the United States of America
Bloomington, Indiana

This book is printed on acid-free paper.

"And behold I send the promise of my Father upon you; but tarry ye in the city of Jerusalem, until ye be endued with power from on high."

(Luke 24:49)

Dedication

I want to dedicate this book to all my brothers and sisters in the Body of Christ, who have been with me and brought much encouragement into my life. May God richly bless you all.

Foreword

Martin Tuson came into our lives some years ago when he saw my husband giving his testimony on Revelation TV. Jezry was sharing about how he got saved in prison. Since then Martin and his wife Margaret and their two girls have become some of our closest friends.

God has used Martin in the prisons of Northern Ireland in such a profound and yet simple way and his many correspondences with prisoners and their response to him is astounding. His prayer of healing as dictated to him by the Holy Spirit has brought healing to many lives in prison and throughout the world. At times he has shared with my husband and me some of these responses and the incredible healing that takes place whenever individuals read and meditate on this prayer.

His first book "Reflection of Christ: God's power inside the prison cell" has been a source of inspiration to many and

I know that this book will be no less so. It is a continuation of the first book and contains many letters of testimony from people as far away as India, people whom he corresponds with or those who have had his healing prayer passed on to them through other inmates. This stands as a testimony to the mighty God that we serve. God truly has remarkable people and uses them in remarkable ways.

We pray that when you read this book you too will come to realize that nothing is impossible when we put our trust in the living God.

Psalm 103:2-4
"Bless the Lord, O my soul,
And forget not all his benefits:
Who forgives all your iniquities,
Who heals all your diseases,
Who redeems your life from destruction,
Who crowns you with loving kindness and tender mercies….."

Jezry and Margaret Harasimowicz
(God's Band)

Introduction

For some time now, it has been on my mind to write another book. It's been quite a while since "Reflection of Christ" was written.

Over these past many years I have been blessed to be a witness to the power of our risen Saviour. Many, many testimonies have been received. I firstly want to thank my precious Lord Jesus Christ for all of the content within the pages of this book. Yes, He receives all of the glory. I believe very strongly that the Lord's anointing is upon this book and that many who read it will be set free from their own afflictions.

The following chapters contain many of the testimonies from individuals both inside and outside of the prison cell. Many of these people (you might be surprised to find out) were not Christians. I have not altered or changed these testimonies in any way. They are written as received. In the Old Testament book of Malachi it says (in chapter 6 verse 3) "I am the Lord God. I never change". Truly God's healing power is very much alive today. This book, though filled with many testimonies, is still but only a small amount of what I have received over these past years.

I believe God's timing is always perfect. I can testify to this so many times in my own life. Please do be encouraged. I know that many will struggle with the contents of this book. Everything you read is a living testimony. To God be all of the glory: great things He has done and continues to do.

Martin Tuson

Acknowledgements

I would like to thank my Sister Gwen Mills for all the hard work and many hours spent in the preparation and typing of this book; to Jezry and Margaret Harasimowicz for writing the Foreword; thanks to my Brother Joe Lockhart for his encouragement and prayers. For all the people who wrote their testimonies etc.

Most of all I want to give all of the praise, glory and honour unto my precious Lord and Saviour Jesus Christ for everything written within the pages of this book.

CONTACT DETAILS

martintuson@tiscali.co.uk

Website www.setfree.free-online.co.uk

Contents

Dedication	vi
Foreword	vii
Introduction	ix
Acknowledgements	xi
Chapter 1 Where did it start?	1
Chapter 2 Kingdom Authority	6
Chapter 3 Greater Works	14
Chapter 4 God's Power in Prison	16
Chapter 5 Testimonies from Pakistan	29
Chapter 6 Angela	36
Chapter 7 Raised from the Dead	38
Chapter 8 Demonstration of Power	40
Chapter 9 I Didn't Believe!	43
Chapter 10 My Heart was Broken	46
Chapter 11 God's Power in India	49
Chapter 12 Delivered from Epilepsy	64
Chapter 13 Hugh's Testimony	67
Chapter 14 Being Bold	71
Chapter 15 Phone Ministry	76
Chapter 16 Only Believe	79
Chapter 17 The name of Jesus	84
Chapter 18 To God be the Glory	90

Chapter I

Where did it start?

Many will know of my calling to serve God within the prison cell. This took place on the 30th June 2000. It was about two years later that I started to pray for the sick. People will ask me today:" Where did it all start?"

Well, just as the Lord gave me a burden to reach out to those within the prison cell, it was a similar experience with my calling to pray for the sick. I started to develop a burden to see individuals touched and healed by the Lord. God started to speak into my life with His still, small voice. He gave me many powerful scriptures; two verses in particular were from the Book of Acts – chapter 4, verses 29 -30.In these verses the Apostle Peter is speaking just after he had been threatened and released by the Sadducees. Peter prays to the Father and says:"And now Lord, behold their threatenings; and grant unto thy servants, that with all boldness they may speak thy word."(verse 30)"By stretching forth thine hand to heal; and that signs and wonders may be done in the name of thy holy child, Jesus."

It was these two verses that God really placed within my heart – so much so that I wrote them out and kept them in my Bible. Each Friday before I would enter into the prison I would read and meditate on these scriptures. I then prayed to the Lord and asked that if anyone came my way on the wings that had a problem with his health, that He would give me boldness to pray for healing and that miracles would manifest. This is exactly what took place. Miracles of healing began. The first miracles I witnessed were within the walls of HM Prison, Maghaberry.

At this point I would like to share a little about healing. Many have mentioned the words "faith healer" to me, especially those who are not born again believers. I am no faith healer. My faith is in God to heal: He is the one who does the healing; I am only a channel. I remember one young inmate asking me how I was able to heal his sickness. I assured him it wasn't me but God who had healed him.

Another question that is always asked is "Why isn't everyone healed?" I cannot answer this, but one thing I want to make clear is this: God is sovereign. We know not everyone will be saved: it's the same with healing. I am a living testimony of God's power to heal.

Again I want to stress that the greatest miracle is the miracle of salvation, which takes place the day a person puts his faith and trust in Christ. I would rather see one man or woman come to Christ than 100 healed in their physical bodies. There is too much negativity today, even within the Body of Christ. Let us concentrate on the positive and on what God is doing.

So I pray for individuals and it is God who heals, for through these miracles His name is being glorified and lifted up. Many times we Christians have felt led to pray with someone. Nine times out of ten we don't do it. Is this not the prompting of God's Holy Spirit? I know. I have been there. Maybe you should just go ahead and pray. You never know, the Lord just might surprise you.

Today I listen to the voice of the Holy Spirit. I will share an example with you. One night in my workplace I contacted a friend by text. His reply was that he was ill with pain in his head. Now the Holy Spirit told me not to phone but to simply text him and say:"In Jesus name you are healed". Now in the flesh you might say don't be so ridiculous. Anyway, I was obedient and text him back a message of healing.

A minute or so later he responded and these are the very words he used:"The pain has gone from my head. I am shaking and there is heat going through my body." So maybe you should listen to God's voice when he speaks to you. Praise him!

I want to share some powerful scriptures on healing. Jeremiah chapter 17 verse 14 says "Heal me, O Lord, and I shall be healed; save me, and I shall be saved; for thou art my praise." Also in Jeremiah chapter 30 verse 17 it says "For I will restore health unto thee, and I will heal thee of thy wounds; saith the Lord." In the book of Exodus chapter

3

23 verse 25 it says "And ye shall serve the Lord your God, and He shall bless thy bread, and thy water; and I will take sickness away from the midst of thee."

Throughout the following chapters you will read testimonies of healing, everything from cancer, Aids, blindness and even the dead being raised back to life again. I will always ask a person to write their testimony of healing. You will read many testimonies through the anointed prayer which the Lord gave me some years back. Be encouraged and if you are suffering yourself from any problems in your health, well I believe that God's healing power will flow into your own situation as you read through this book.

I want to end this chapter with a poem that was written by Sister Isabelle from Durham. I prayed for her whilst I was in Durham ministering. She has written her testimony in the form of a poem.

Testimony:Isabelle

One Saturday afternoon
I went to see a man, named Martin Tuson
From Northern Ireland he came
To spread God's word
To Eunice's house, we rallied about
To hear this man who spoke the word of God.
For healing I came
For my back was in pain.
With healing hands laid on my spine
He sent prayers and praises to God.
With the heat of his hand, my spine grew warm
As he prayed over me, for healing from God
It worked in me. When the praying stopped
I stood there shaking; I could not stop.
After 13 years of pain I could bend down again.
I touched my toes, I touched the floor
And I could do a whole lot more.
So I dance and sing for joy
For the works that God can do.
He is so majestic, wonderful,
An awesome God to know.
I walk with Him everyday,
Singing His praises on the way.
So Martin Tuson with the healing from God
A healer for the people through the word of our God.
Always walk in God's footsteps, and He will always be there,
His love raining down over us.
So just take care to say a prayer
And thank the Lord for what He gives us everyday.

Testimony from Sister Isabelle
June 19th 2007

Chapter 2

Kingdom Authority

"And when He had called unto Him His twelve disciples, He gave unto them power against unclean spirits, to cast them out and to heal all manner of sickness and all manner of disease." **(Matthew 10 verse 1)**

The following testimonies are from individuals who I have prayed for. Praise God for each one of them. As born again believers we have been given Kingdom authority over all sickness and illness. To God be all the glory.

Dear Martin,

I had been suffering from asthma since the age of 13, brought on by the stress of my Father's death. From then to now I have been in hospitals several times and seen many doctors. I was given medication and had to take inhalers twice a day.

I also was suffering with pain in my chest, back and sides. I'd have to stop to catch my breath while out walking. My fiancé, Jonathan, became a Christian while in Maghaberry Prison. He told me about you Martin and how he prayed to meet you, and he did meet you. Jonathan gave you my number and you rang me that day.

You prayed down the phone for me and the pain was gone almost immediately. From that day until now I have had no pain at all and it is a relief to be able to walk without stopping all the time. I am so happy that you rang me that day and that I was touched by the Lord who healed me.

Jonathan is really happy and has changed so much over the last few weeks. Becoming a Christian has changed his life completely for the better. You inspire him so much, Martin. Thank you and God bless!

Maria

Dear Martin,

I have to tell you about a miracle God worked for my sister Brenda. She was working for the army and they were training the troops, getting them ready to go to Iraq. One day a very large young man accidentally ran into her and knocked her down.

Her shoulder was injured and she was in severe pain and was on strong medication. She could hardly get out of bed and could not do her housework or anything else. About four days after it happened she phoned me. She was crying because she was in so much pain. She said the pills were not doing any good and that she could not go on. I ran into my bedroom where I have your healing prayer on the wall. I started praying that prayer for her and she was praising God and crying at the same time. When I finished she moved her arm and shoulder and was crying even more. She said her arm didn't hurt any more and that she was healed. We both gave God all the glory. It was her back, arm and shoulder that had been injured and now she was totally healed. Praise Jesus!

She went back to her doctor and told him that Jesus had healed her. He said: "Now, that's what I like to hear". We are telling everyone about this miracle.

....

My husband met a man called Martin Tuson. He is a born again Christian. My husband, George, and I are both believers. My husband went to talk to Martin about witnessing for the Lord in Maghaberry Prison. My husband had been suffering with a lot of pain in his shoulder. He had had a bad fall a few weeks previous to this.

Martin prayed for my husband and put his hand on his shoulder. When he finished praying, George had no pain and could lift his arm up for the first time in two weeks. The Lord healed George through Martin. The Lord truly uses Martin in praying for the sick. Glory to our God and Saviour.

Geordie then came home and told me about all that had happened. I told him that I wanted the Lord to heal me from an illness in my spine. I had suffered three years with this and was in a lot of pain. I had prayed often for the Lord to heal me. No doctor could ever cure it, but the Lord is the greatest doctor of all. I asked my husband if Martin would pray for me. He said "Esther, I will pray for you and use the healing prayer in Martin's booklet." When he placed his hands on my back I felt a warm sensation and the pain started to move. It had never done this before. I then got the sensation that I needed to go to the toilet. Then all of the pain left me. It was gone.

Thank you, Lord.

....

Martin, you made a house visit to me on Friday 26 August 2006 and prayed for me and laid hands on me. I was grieving for my late husband and trying to cut out anti depressant tablets. I stopped them on Saturday and was off them for ten days and was feeling much better. I was then prescribed an alternative anti depressant and took only five of them before stopping them altogether. I am on nothing now.

I believe your prayers in conjunction with my ceasing to take tablets has been the Lord working for me because the next day after your visit I felt more at ease than ever before.

Thank you for your time and ministry.
Doreen

....

In January I phoned Martin on his mobile about his ministry. During the conversation Martin asked me about my illness, as he knew I had thrombosis in both legs. I had severe pain in my right lower calf in the main artery where the hospital gave me injections to disperse a clot that had formed. After this I was left with severe pain. I couldn't straighten my leg or put any pressure on it while standing straight. Martin began to pray for me and within minutes I was able to get up, bend my leg backwards and forwards and walk with no problem. This is not the first time Martin has blessed me with his healing powers. In November 2005 he phoned me about his ministry work and once again asked me how I was keeping. When I said I had severe abdominal pain he told me to place my hand on my stomach as he prayed for me. Soon afterwards, while we were still on the phone, the pain disappeared and I was able to breathe properly. As you can see by these two testimonies, Martin has been chosen by our Saviour to minister to the sick and those who have been incarcerated. Martin is simply Jesus' right hand man!

God bless you Martin with your ministry.

Barry Owens

....

In January 2006 I pulled a muscle at the bottom of my back. I was in a lot of pain and could not walk straight. At the end of January Martin phoned my husband to talk about his ministry and my husband asked Martin to pray for me over the phone. Martin told me to put my hand on my back. As he prayed I felt heat on my back. Martin then asked me to stand up. I couldn't believe it: I was standing straight and had no pain. I was feeling great but a few days later I tripped on some steps and hurt my back again. A short time later I was in Martin's company and I asked him to pray for me again as the pain was so severe I couldn't reach to the floor or walk about. Martin then prayed with me to put my back right again. He told me to reach down and touch my toes and then stand up. I was able to do this with no problems and thanks to the grace of God I have had no problems since then.

Thank you Lord and bless Martin in his ministries.

Lorraine Owens

....

My baby daughter Jenna had a virus which resulted in her having wart like spots on her arms, legs and trunk. We asked the advice of three medical people as to what we could do for her. We were told the virus could last for up to nine or ten months unless we burst the spots and scrubbed them with a nail brush! We did this once and it caused Jenna great trauma and actually didn't affect the spots at all. We could do nothing and the spots were spreading.

Mum had told me about Martin who had been given the gift of healing. Martin came to our house. He used no magic formula and didn't even touch Jenna, but simply prayed that she would be healed "in Jesus name". A week went by and there was no evidence of any change. Exactly a week after Martin prayed I was thinking negative thoughts and I believe God interrupted my thoughts and said "I have healed Jenna." From then on I chose to believe and had faith that the virus had gone. I also told two of my friends that Jenna had been healed. Three days later we were at Mount Stewart with one of these friends. I went to change Jenna and was amazed at what I saw. Most of the spots that had covered her tummy were gone and the rest had turned into scabs and were just falling off! We were all shocked. During the following week the healing continued and now she only has four left on her arm. What could have lasted nine or ten months, God healed in the space of three weeks!

Our whole family has grown in faith as we have seen the power of our mighty God. God really is the same yesterday, today and for ever. Praise Him!

Thank you Martin for taking the time to pray with us. May you be encouraged and continue to do a great work for God's glory.

Rhonda.

....

Hey martin, I'm sorry it's taken me so long to get this done. I just want to say thanks again for praying for me at

Rend. *For a few days things were still pretty bad with the IBS (Irritable Bowel Syndrome) but now I can eat anything I want to and haven't had any pain since that night. God is so good!*

Anyway, here it is……………………………………………..

My name is Holly and I am 21 years old. Almost a year ago I travelled to Uganda with a Christian youth group. I was there for one month. While I was out there I had the usual stomach upsets most travellers get abroad, but when I got home to Northern Ireland things didn't get any better.

I started getting cramps in my stomach; this got worse and worse and pretty soon I was bloated up every time I ate. This caused a lot of pain in my stomach and back. Certain foods caused the pain and I was fast running out of foods that didn't cause this reaction. The doctor did tests and told me I had Irritable Bowel Syndrome, probably caused by worms I had picked up in Africa. The drugs he gave me didn't have any effect.

One night after about seven months of a very restricted diet, Martin prayed over me at a youth event. My stomach was hurting badly that night and for a few days nothing much seemed to happen, but I kept praying for God to heal me. After a few days the pain was gone and it's now been about two months since that prayer and I can now eat whatever I want. God has completely healed the Irritable Bowel Syndrome. Praise the Lord.

…………………………………..

Chapter 3

Greater Works

"Verily, verily, I say unto you, 'He that believeth on me, the works that I do shall he do also; and greater works than these shall he do because I go unto my Father' ".
(John 14:12)

I remember one year I was on holiday with my family in Salou. We arrived after a short flight. My youngest daughter cried the whole way over. Both my wife and I were stressed out. We ended up being allocated an apartment which we were not happy about. You know at times we can get angry, even with the Lord. I remember looking up to Heaven and saying to the Lord: "Lord you did not send me over here to have all this hassle."

After the usual arguments, we were too tired to argue any more. While we were checking in, I overheard a lady in front of me voicing her anger. "I do not need this; this could be my son's last holiday." Margaret my wife looked at me; she knew what I was thinking. This lady had a five year old son called Ross; he was ill with a bowel complaint. I prayed that night for God to open up a door for me to talk to his mum.

The next morning I got that chance. I asked Amanda about her son and his condition. She told me that the doctors were even reluctant for him to go on holiday. After this two week break, Ross was booked in for major surgery. He was in pain every day and could not even go to the toilet properly; he was also being sick. I told Amanda that I was a Christian and that I believed in God's healing power because I had been a witness to many miracles. I asked her if I might pray for her son and she assured me she would try anything to see him well.

So I took it upon myself to pray for young Ross each night. A few days passed before I met Amanda again. She looked at me in awe and said that from the first night I had started to pray with Ross he had stopped asking for pain relief medication as he did not have any pain. She also said that he was going to the toilet normally. Praise God!

Many weeks later I received a text message from Amanda telling me that Ross did not have to have the operation after all. I believe that is why God sent me to those apartments, praise His Holy Name. What a powerful testimony! The testimonies in the following chapter show God's grace and mercy upon individuals

....

Chapter 4

God's Power in Prison

"And I will bring the blind by a way that they knew not;
I will lead them in paths that they have not known; I will
make darkness light before them and crooked things straight.
These things will I do unto them and not forsake them."
(Isaiah 42:16)

As many of you know, I have been a true witness to the power of our risen Saviour within the prison cell. God's power and love is being demonstrated throughout many prisons in the world today. The following testimonies of healing are all from within the prison cell.

My brother, let me tell you about the time in Lusaka when I tested positive for HIV/Aids. I remained silent and didn't tell you. I took a card which you had sent me and kneeled down and prayed that the words on the card might be true for me. In a short time I was transferred here to Kabwe and I went for tests again because in Lusaka I tested positive. But here in Kabwe, my brother, a miracle happened and I tested negative and I remain negative to this day. So that is why I am taking time to write to you. I believe in your prayers and know that if you pray for me something will happen.

> *God bless you.*
> *Your brother in Christ,*
> *Chrispin Banda*

....

Tues 8th August 2006

Martin, you are an amazing brother in Christ and I count it an honour and blessing to have you as a friend. God has been moving here in Martin House, Maghaberry since you were last here; on two separate occasions God has healed Sammy. One day, Sammy tore a muscle or tendon in his shoulder; even coughing was agony for him. I asked him if I could pray with him and he agreed, so I prayed and held his shoulder. He said that heat went into his shoulder, praise God. A few days later he over- exerted himself and tore it again. I prayed again and God healed him. He's going to write his testimony out for me – he also said that he knows he needs to be right with God. Amen!

> *Joe*

....

Brother Martin,

I greet you in the name of Our Lord Jesus Christ; I want to share my testimony with you. I have had a heart problem since childhood and this used to give me a lot of problems. The problem persisted as I got older. One day one of the other inmates invited me to attend a meeting in Cell 4. I was given a prayer coupon and they prayed for me. Two days later my heart started functioning normally and I have never had the same problem since then. I attribute my heart's healing to the Lord Jesus Christ. Please continue sending prayer anointed coupons so that many more people can be healed.

May the Lord richly bless you.
Yours sincerely,
Andrew Tembo

....

Beloved Brother Martin,

Greetings in the mighty name of our Lord Jesus Christ. I was delighted to receive your letter and the word of God. As for me, I am doing fine and can not complain. Brother Martin, the Lord has been so gracious and merciful to us. He continues to perform wonders through the healing prayers you are sending.

People here are appreciating the work that I am doing to deliver the written Word of God. One of the inmates had suffered with a swollen leg for some time and God performed a miracle for him. Upon praying the healing prayer, the inmate who had not been able to walk for some weeks, was able to walk again. The patient attributed this healing to the prayers that had been made for him. He is now walking without pain or any problems and we continue praising God for His healing power.

Yours in Christ
Br. Chrispin Banda

....

One Friday afternoon Martin called over to the Education block, as usual to visit me and give spiritual guidance. On that particular day I had severe headaches and pain in my neck as well. (at that time I worked in the Braille Unit and often sat at a PC screen for hours on end.) I happened to mention this to Martin and he asked to pray for me. As he started to pray I felt a heavy burden lift up from my shoulders. The best way to describe it is this - it was like a warm feeling coming over me along with a calm which I had not felt in a very long time. On another occasion something similar happened to me. It was a special service one Sunday in the prison chapel. Martin announced that he would pray for all who had health or personal problems. As he started to pray I could feel the pain in my back start to ease and I was able to walk upright without any problems. Since then I have been able to cut down on the number of pain killers needed. On a personal level I have no doubt our Lord was present on both occasions and also that God is using Martin as an instrument for His good works.

Trevor

....

Dear Martin

I would like to use this medium to introduce myself briefly. My name is Douglas Ncube, an inmate in a Thai prison.   I got your address from your powerful and miraculous booklet. A friend of mine John Charles shared it with me. I was healed through it and that is why it is imperative that I write you my testimony.

I had been suffering with an excruciating pain in my left knee; it had been troubling me for about six months. It was causing me a lot of discomfort and there was no medical remedy. A few days ago I shared with John about this persistent problem. He promised to give me an antidote the next day. I was very curious to know what he was going to give me, but he did not go into any details. The next day he gave me your healing prayer, as promised. I reluctantly accepted it, but without any intention of using it. Later in my room I changed my mind and decided to try it.   That night I prayed fervently over my problem with your healing prayer and I was healed instantly. Now I can run without any pain and this miracle has increased my faith in the Lord Jesus Christ.

Thank you dear Brother Martin. I will soon be transferring back to my own country and it will be an opportunity to share with others in my country about your healing prayer.

....

As a Christian in prison I enjoy fund raising events to help people less fortunate than myself. On 17th March 2005 I was planning to run a marathon to raise money for the N Ireland Chest Heart and Stroke Association.

As my training intensified I picked up injuries on my feet. One week before my run my feet were in complete agony with blisters and bruises. I was convinced my marathon was over before it even started.

My dear friend Martin visited me one Friday afternoon five days before my run. We chatted for a while and I then told him about the situation with my feet. We prayed a short, meaningful prayer asking our Father in Heaven to heal and bless my feet.

I then took off one of my socks; my bruises were not black or swollen, just red in colour. I stepped up to walk and there was no pain. We praised God, our Lord for this miracle.

I was able to run my marathon and raise funds for the charity.

Paul

....

On Friday 14th October 2005 I asked Martin to say a prayer for me because of the pain I had in my neck. Martin had prayed for me some months earlier when I was having trouble with my left shoulder and since then I have never had *any trouble with it. Last Friday he prayed for me again and since then my neck has been pain free.*

D Brown

....

Last week the Lord healed my panic attacks and I am on the way to recovery. I feel a lot better since my meeting with Martin and the Lord has assured me I am healed through my prayer time and I have no doubts.

Tony

....

Joe Dziwa's testimony (Livingstone prison)

Hello,

My name is Joe Dziwa, an inmate serving seven years for robbery. I have been incarcerated for four years now and I am due for release in 2008. During my imprisonment I have been battling with pulmonary tuberculosis. I am drug resistant and have been on about three treatment courses but all to no avail. The disease used to disappear for a while and then re- appear within a few months. This resulted in my body becoming weak and thin.

What happened last month was astonishing. A group of believers visited our prison to minister and pray for the sick. When I heard about them I went there and they prayed for me using a healing prayer which they said came directly from God. I could not believe them but because I was in pain I knelt down and they laid hands on my head and asked me to believe God for my healing. When they had finished I felt my body become lighter and was surprised to discover that I had even gained strength. Now two weeks later, I feel fine. My coughing has stopped and I have started gaining weight, much to the surprise of everybody. I have since repented and am now a born again Christian, because Jesus has shown His mercy even to me a sinner. He can do the same for you, if you only believe.

....

I am Davies Sichinga. I have not been feeling well for the past week. I was diagnosed as suffering from malaria and was given a drug called fancida. I was hesitant to take this drug because it is very strong and people say it even makes the illness worse. Then I met Edwin and his friends Roger and Martin. I remained with Edwin while Roger went to get another sick inmate.

When Edwin prayed for me I felt well and all the body pains stopped. It is really amazing because the other guy who was prayed for also claimed to have been healed. We talked at length and I have really been inspired. I will continue following the Lord with my whole heart. I have even joined a choir group because I feel like singing for the Lord.

Davies Sichinga
18/0/06 censored

....

I'm Dalias Chewe. I am 50 years old. I am a male convict at a maximum security prison. I committed murder. I have been suffering from headaches most of the time. I was told that there was a group of young men who had started praying for the sick prisoners met on Thursdays, but before I could look for these guys as there are many men in this prison, Edwin came and found me lying down. He asked me if I believed in healing by Jesus Christ. I said yes I believe He can heal the sick because when He was here on earth He healed those who were sick and the dead were brought back to life. He had a small prayer in his hands and told me he was going to pray for me. When he prayed I felt well; the headaches disappeared. Praise be to God who heals.

Dalias Chewe
18/01/06 censored

....

My name is Simon Simbeye. I am 86 years old and I am in a maximum security prison serving 15 years for the offence of defilement, a crime I didn't even commit. I was severely beaten by the villagers when they heard that I wanted to marry a small girl. Because of the beating I have been suffering from chest pains for four years.

One day someone informed me that there was a group of people who were praying for their fellow inmates and that some of the sick were being healed. I went there and they prayed for me. Two of these men of God put their hands on my head. I came to know their names later; the first one is Roger and the second one is Edwin. I thank God that the pain I was feeling stopped immediately. I now believe there is a God who heals.

Simon Simbeye

....

Beloved brother Martin,

God bless you Martin. Great news my brother; three of the inmates who had HIV/Aids have been back to the hospital for new tests. You sent each one of them an anointed healing cloth and told them to keep it on their person at all times. Praise God Martin, their tests came back negative. God has healed them. Thank you for the cloths you sent to them. Praise Him for these wonderful miracles.

Pastor Matthews

....

I wanted to write to you, brother, about the healing miracles which took place. My brother, I am sorry to say that I did not believe in your healing prayers at the start. But I have to admit that God is working in a miraculous way, praise Him. There were two inmates in this Thai prison who received a copy of your healing prayer. I could not understand why they were so zealous.

I must say I always carried your prayer with me at all times but sadly I denied it. My inner spirit kept telling me to use it. So back in my room after 9 pm one night something woke me from my sleep. It is difficult to express what this was. I immediately read your healing prayer. I felt something different in me but could not accept this until the following day. I noticed relief from my abdominal pain; it felt strange within me. I went straight to the two inmates to acknowledge my healing through the healing prayer. The truth was told. Praise God. No more medication was needed. I was forced to express my experience in proclaiming how prayer does marvelous works. I still can't understand it fully.

My brother, it would be so good if it would be possible for you to come and visit Thai prisons to pray for the sick and see them saved.

....

1 April 2006

Hello Martin,

First and foremost, many thanks to Almighty God who has made it possible for me to put pen to paper. How is life treating you there in Bangor? It is my heart's prayer that this letter finds you in excellent spirit and health. As for me, I am feeling much better both spiritually and physically.

Several months ago I wrote to you requesting a prayer cloth for my eyesight as I was blind. I received the prayer cloth on 30th November 2005 with an open mind and heart. Thanks! It brings me great joy and hope to tell you that my prayers have been answered and a miracle has occurred. Many have been praying for me and my eyesight has been returning gradually. What I didn't know was that I had been blind in my left eye for about five years before I lost my eyesight completely. My doctor recently gave me an eye examination and discovered that not only is my vision returning in my right eye, but I can see with my left eye as well. I am now able to see colours.

The eyesight problem is now fully healed and the prayer cloth has been passed on to someone with the same type of problem. I used the prayer cloth for three months. I carried it in my pocket all day and slept on it during the night. The results were quickly and gratefully received. The Lord is good and looks after us very well.

I pray that God will continue to shower you with unlimited blessings. Always trust in God knowing He never fails. (Isaiah

41:10) You are much in my thoughts and prayers. God bless you abundantly. I look forward to hearing from you soon.

    Yours faithfully
    Owen

           ....

Chapter 5

Testimonies from Pakistan

"The Lord Thy God in the midst of thee is mighty: He will save, He will rejoice over thee with joy; He will rest in his love, He will joy over thee with singing." (Zephaniah 3:17)

One day I received a letter from a brother in Christ called Mark Amir who lives in Punjab, Pakistan. He had heard about my ministry and he wrote:

"Brother, I have to be involved in this great ministry." This was the start of a correspondence between Mark and me. He was a young evangelist, filled with the Holy Spirit and on fire for God. I am blessed to know this young man. I encouraged him to start praying for the sick and sent our literature to him. I also sent our booklet 'Nothing is Impossible' along with copies of the anointed healing prayer. Mark started praying for the sick using this prayer and God healed many people.

He e-mailed me about the booklet 'Nothing is Impossible'. This booklet contains 42 testimonies of God's healing power: many thousands of booklets have been printed. God worked many amazing miracles of healing through this anointed book, which also contained the healing prayer. Brother Mark thought it would be a powerful book to have translated into the Urdu language for those in Pakistan. He spent a lot of time on the Urdu production of the book and this soon became a reality. Two thousand copies were produced and many were touched by God's power as they read through the book. Mark represents our Ministry in Pakistan. God's Spirit is upon this work in a mighty way.

The following testimonies which Mark has e-mailed me, are all from Pakistan; I thank God for the move of His Spirit there.

....

Date: 16/06/2007
Subject: Naveed Islamabad

Dear Brother Martin Tuson

Greetings.

My name is Naveed and I am quite young; I am working as a Visa officer in the Thai Embassy in Islamabad, Pakistan. I had been suffering from fever, which caused me bleeding from the mouth and nose; the fever usually lasted a fortnight at a time. My work was suffering because of my poor health as I was so often on sick leave. Fortunately evangelist Mark Amir prayed for me using the prescribed prayer revealed to you in 'Nothing is Impossible'.

I am glad to say I at once felt tremendous energy in my body and the fever left at once. I no longer suffer from fever and enjoy good health once again. By the grace of God I can work on a regular basis. I thank the Lord Jesus, Evangelist Mark Amir and you. I believe Mark is truly anointed with healing power and is an honest and faithful servant of God. May God reward and bless you Brother Martin, too.

In His Love
Naveed
Islamabad, Pakistan

....

Date: 03/06/2007
Subject: Blind Man's Testimony

Brother Martin,
Last week I visited a family in my home city, Sahiwal. There was a young man there who was suffering from eye trouble. He had been unable to see for the previous three months. His family were greatly worried about this. They had contacted a doctor but nothing could be done for him medically. They took the young man to some people for prayer and gave them a lot of money to have his eyesight restored, but it was no use. When I arrived they asked me to pray for him. I read your healing prayer to him that evening and I

31

also asked a family member who could read to say the prayer for him again. Two hours later he was able to see a little. The next morning he could see completely. Praise God for His healing power; now he can see.

Praise God for the great miracle that happened here.

Mark

....

Date: 03/06/2007
Subject: Younas Testimony

Dear Brother Martin,

Greetings! I am grateful to you and Brother Mark for giving me your book and the healing prayer. My name is Younas and I am living here in Sahiwal in Pakistan. I am 57 years old and have a heart problem which has persisted for four years despite all the medication I have taken. Mark Amir prayed for me and also gave me a copy of the healing prayer. I read it and continue to read it even now. I got my medical check-up and reports showed that I had improved. I am well now. God healed me through your healing prayer and blessed me through your book also. I am feeling good. Praise His holy name!

Younas,
Sahiwal, Pakistan

....

Date: 16/08/2006
Subject: God Bless you

Respected Brother Martin,
Greetings! I am thankful to you for your kind reply. This is a testimony of a man called Ishafiq Masih, who injured his left eye five years ago. His eye was red and very painful. I used your prayer and God healed him completely. I will send you his photograph. He is now completely healed.
Your brother in Christ,
Mark

....

Date: 27/9/2006
Subject: Testimony

Yesterday I prayed for a sister who called me because she was very worried and was crying and crying. She had been to see a doctor at the clinic but he was not able to help her. Then she called me and I prayed for her. Yesterday she called me back and said she was completely healed from her sickness by the power of God.
Praise God,
Amen

....

Date: 30/08/2006
Subject: One More Testimony
This happened to a fifty year old lady called Sheraffin Ramzian. She is married and has three children. There was some problem in her house and she became sick and had been paralysed for some time. I went to the hospital to meet her.

She was very worried about her children. She could not move her hand and she was crying out to God for healing. I asked her if she believed in Jesus and she said she did. I then asked her if she believed that Jesus could heal her and she replied that only Jesus could heal her. Then I prayed for her in the spirit, right there in the hospital.

I saw the power of God touch her and she was completely healed. Praise God for the great work He did. Now she can move her hand and eat by herself. Since she has gone home she can do the cooking again. Her husband and children and surprised at what God has done. They have promised they will worship God and His son Jesus Christ.

....

Date: 30/08/2006
Subject: Nila

An 8ᵗʰ year student called Nila was being disturbed by some devil spirits working in her life. They took her to the Hindu temple and tried to get healing from their gods but they could not help her. They paid money for healing but the evil spirits said they would not leave and that they would destroy her life. Her family brought her to my house for prayer.

I asked the family if they believed in Jesus Christ but they were not true Christians. They repented of their sins, confessed and then gave their lives to God. I prayed for them and God healed their daughter. Now she is released from the evil spirits and she is now very happy and promising to serve God. They worship God and pray to Him every day.

....

Date: 06/11/2006
Subject: Anslem

Dear Brother Martin,

Greetings. My name is Anslem Saleem Anwar and I am from the same city as Brother Mark. I had been suffering from sickness and weakness for a few weeks and had a fever. Brother Mark visited me. He prayed for me and gave me a copy of the healing prayer. I read it again and again. Soon the fever left me. I am on my way to a speedy recovery of health.

I thank the Lord for healing me. I am thankful to Brother Mark for giving me this prayer letter. I believe that Jesus is the same yesterday, today and for ever.

God bless you Brother Martin
Thanks for the prayer,
Anslem

....

Chapter 6

Angela

"And Jesus looking upon them said: with men it is impossible
but not with God; for with God all things are possible"
(Mark 10:27)

The following testimony is a wonderful story of God's
grace and healing power. For many years I have been writing
to my brother Chrispin Banda, an inmate in a maximum
security prison in Zambia. Chrispin has been touched
many times by God's healing power; he too has been a
witness to Christ's power.

He wrote to me some time ago and shared with me
that his daughter Angela was in Lusaka Central Hospital.
He was totally distraught. Apparently she had fallen out
of a tree and broken her pelvis. The main problem was
that the medical staff could not stop the flow of blood from

her private parts. Chrispin asked me to send her a healing prayer.

When I send prayers or anointed cloths out I always lay hands on them and pray over them in the name of Jesus. I did this with one of the anointed healing prayers. Amazingly when I took my hand off this prayer, the paper had my hand print on it. I knew straight away that God would touch and heal Angela. I sent her the prayer and later received the following testimony from her. Praise God once again for His power.

"Uncle Martin Tuson,
Greetings in the name of our God. Daddy has asked me to write and tell you what God has done for me. This is my testimony.

I had fallen from a tree and was taken to Lusaka Central Hospital. I was losing blood through my private parts and was in great pain. That's when I received your prayer. My grandmother read it over me and placed it under my pillow. That night as I was sleeping I saw a great light and I felt someone touch my abdomen. I screamed but no-one heard me. When I woke up the pain was gone and the flow of blood had stopped. I felt that I needed to go to the toilet. My grandmother wanted to help me but I insisted on going on my own. I was completely healed. The doctors were amazed at what had happened. I was sent home. After I was discharged I went to visit my father in prison. He was amazed too. So I was healed through prayer medicine from heaven written on white paper. My dad told me to pray and go to church. God Bless you."
Your niece,
Angela Banda

Chapter 7

Raised from the Dead

"The blind receive their sight and the lame walk, the lepers are cleansed and the deaf hear, the dead are raised up, and the poor have the gospel preached to them." (Matthew 11:5)

Today throughout the world, God is still raising people from the dead. I have many testimonies that show this. I want to add that the following testimony is a true and living one. It is from Pastor P Premakumur in India and is dated 2/11/2006. This pastor used the anointed healing prayer on Mr K Raja Rao.

The man named K Raja Rao is aged 30 years, married and has two children. He has no job; there are no jobs for educated men in India. He suffered deprivation of food and clothing for many years. He faced many difficulties in his life; because there was no food he sent his wife and two children away to her parents. He searched for work in hotels, workshops, fishing trawlers, buses, cleaning but there was no work of any kind. Day by day his situation was very depressing with no wife, no children, no one to care for him, very little food.

In this very dark situation he drank poison and died. Doctors did their best and gave him many medicines to try to make him vomit but there was no life in him. At that time Pastor P Premakumar visited him and found no life in him. By faith he prayed and used your anointed prayer. He put the paper on his heart and prayed in the powerful name of Jesus. The dead man came to life. God did this miracle right there in the hospital. He is still weak but is gaining strength day by day. He has accepted Christ as his Saviour and Lord and dedicated his life to work with our pastor P Premakumar. His wife has come back. He is distributing tracts to all kinds of people and serving the Lord full time. Please pray for him and his family.

P Premakumar
Mulagada Housing Colony.

Chapter 8

Demonstration of Power

*"For the preaching of the cross is to them that perish
foolishness; but unto us which are saved it is the power of
God" (1 Corinthians Ch1 vs18)*

I had been asked to speak at a youth meeting one
Saturday night. The age group ranged from 17 to 25. I
remember particularly that night that I wasn't in the best
form to take a meeting, but God still uses us despite the way
we feel at times.

When we arrived at the church hall that night I remember
how cold it was. There were about 30 chairs set out ready
for the meeting. I went into one of the rooms to spend some
time in prayer before the meeting started. I still had my coat
on and didn't take it off the whole meeting. I came back into
the hall and to my surprise, the room was alive and bursting

with young folk. So much for the 30 or so seats; there were more like 70 or 80 people there. God already knew what He was going to do that night. The music was loud but it was great to watch those young people praising and lifting their voices to the Lord.

When my time to speak came I spoke on the Book of Acts Chapters 2-4. I shared about the disciples and the fact that they were ignorant and unlearned men, but they had encountered the Messiah. When you have an encounter with the living God things have to change. I explained to them that I too could relate to the disciples, being ignorant and unlearned myself, but when these rough and rugged men were filled with the Holy Spirit, they changed the world with the gospel of Jesus Christ.

I said to them that I could speak all night and share one testimony after another of God's power but that I wanted them to affect their families and friends and see miracles manifested. I prayed for boldness for these young people. At the end of the meeting I asked anyone who had a need in their health or any other area to come forward. As in other meetings, people did not rush to the front. A young girl with a problem in her hands and arms came forward. I prayed for healing and God's power touched and healed her.

Then many more came for prayer. There must have been 30 – 40 young people who came to the front. A young man stood waiting for prayer. He said: "Martin, I sat the whole time you spoke in complete agony. I have a slipped disc in my back." I placed my hands over the area of the disc and prayed. I felt something move as I prayed. When I asked him how he felt he started to cry. The disc had moved back into place and he was completely healed by the power of God. He hugged me with tears in his eyes and then bent over and touched his toes. He was running all around the hall that night praising God for this miracle.

Many others were healed that night. God's power was really demonstrated as problems with shin splints, muscle injuries, wrist injuries and shoulder injuries were all healed. In all there were ten miracles of healing. Even though I was not feeling up to it, God still used me in that condition to see His name glorified and lifted up. Praise His Holy Name. It was a night that I will never forget. Weeks after the meeting I was receiving testimonies of people who were healed. I believe that many of these young people were blessed and encouraged that night. What a Mighty God we serve.

Chapter 9

I Didn't Believe!

"For the Kingdom of God is not in word but in power"
(I Corinthians Ch 4 V 20)

The following testimony involves an inmate from Perth Prison in Scotland.

George was not a Christian and did not have any real belief in God's power to heal. I came to know him through another inmate, Ricky. Ricky suggested that because like me, George was from Ireland there might be some sort of connection between us. At the start when Ricky asked him if he would like to write to me he showed no interest. I think he did not like the idea of a Christian writing to him.

Anyway, he finally agreed and I sent him a letter. As I do with most first letters, I sent along some of our literature and included a copy of our little booklet "Nothing is Impossible".

This little booklet is a miracle in itself as so many people have been healed by God's power through it.

I posted this off to George but weeks passed and I did not receive a reply. Then one day Ricky phoned to say George had a letter in the post for me. It seemed he had something to share with me which amazed him. I will let you read George's letter for yourself. Now remember, this man was not a Christian and did not believe in God's healing power. George writes:

"Dear Martin,

Firstly I apologize for not being in touch sooner as I have a lot to thank you for, my friend. The reason I haven't written sooner is that I find it hard to trust people. I don't know if Ricky told you about my situation, but, I've been through a lot. I realize you are a genuine person and again I am sorry for not writing back.

The reason I say I have a lot to thank you for is this – please don't laugh as I myself find it hard to believe, but you can ask Ricky. I have had problems with my hand for about nine months. I could not bend my thumb or wrist and was in some discomfort the whole time. I applied various creams but none of them worked. When you wrote to me and sent in something called a healing prayer, I was so frustrated that nothing had helped my hand that I decided I might as well try it. To be honest I didn't think it would do any good as my wrist was so damaged. Now it didn't happen straight away but I said the prayer every night and kept it inside my pillowcase. After just over a week though, the problem had completely gone. I don't know if it was just a coincidence, but

I doubt it as I had been suffering for nine months, then within a week it was healed. So for that I thank you, Martin."

Through this miracle George knew that God was real and later on he received the Lord into his life. What about that for God's grace and mercy? I tell you, the Lord can break into the hardest of hearts. Praise Him!

Chapter 10

My Heart was Broken

"Make haste, O God, to deliver me: make haste to help me, O Lord." (Psalm 70:1)

Over these past five years or so I have been so blessed to be a witness to the power of our Risen Saviour. When I speak or minister at different meetings, I always pray for the sick. Every single time, God's power is there to heal and make whole.

Just recently I was ministering in Durham and Newcastle. It was an amazing two days. Many were healed. In Durham I prayed for some people who had come along to my sister in Christ, Eunice's home. They all had come for healing. God's presence and power flowed that Saturday afternoon. In chapter 1 you will read one of the testimonies from that afternoon - Isabelle's testimony. God was touching people one after another. One woman had problems with her back and shoulder. She had endured fifteen years of pain in her back and two years of pain in her shoulder. She was overcome when God healed her instantly. Her husband was also healed from a shoulder injury.

A lady with Motor Neuron disease was touched by God's power. It was a wonderful two days and God's name was lifted high and exalted in all that took place. A few weeks after I arrived home I had the privilege of leading an alcoholic to the Lord. He had read my literature which I had left at Durham. John experienced God's love and received Christ into his life.

I thank God that though our literature many miracles are taking place. It says in Romans 1:16 "the power of God unto salvation" through the miracles, signs and wonders, the greatest miracle of all is taking place. Individuals are putting their trust in Christ and receiving Him into their lives. You may be reading this book now and you are not a born again Christian. My prayer is that you will bow the knee this very day and put your trust in Christ. What a joy to be in God's family.

What you are reading in this book should be enough proof to convince you that God is real and that He loves you. Even now as you are reading this chapter I sense that God is speaking to your heart. Just simply ask Him to forgive you and ask Him into your heart and life as your Personal Saviour. If you pray from a sincere heart He will answer your prayer.

I want to end this chapter with another powerful testimony of healing from Geofrey Zimba, Zambia.

"Dear Martin,

As a little child I suffered so much that I would look up to the stars and beg God, who I thought might be up there somewhere, to take me away from the earth. I was so tired. A great wall of pain seemed to separate me from the pleasures enjoyed by others and I could not explain how I felt because no one could understand. Years passed and I saw my earthly happiness swept away. My heart was broken and I did not know what to do. I cried for help day after day and night after night, although I was not sure if God existed or where He could be found. I only knew that I suffered and was in need of help. I was unable to cope with it all and found myself in despair. This was my condition when I started reading the Healing Prayer. Believe me; I was ready for its message. Within two weeks I was completely healed. Praise be to God, amen. All pain left me and I had a glimpse of the New Heavens and a New Earth.

Geofrey Zimba "

Chapter II

God's Power in India

"But ye shall receive power after that the Holy Ghost is come upon you; and ye shall be witnesses unto Me both in Jerusalem, and in all Judea, and in Samaria and unto the uttermost part of the earth. " (Acts 1:8)

I thank the Lord for finally being able to share this chapter with you. It has always been on my heart to share the following true testimonies from India. In 2006 I got involved with a pastor in India who had planted 20 churches in the Andre Pradesh area, all within a 100 mile radius.

When I first wrote to Pastor Devesahayam I included a letter for him to read over his pastors. I sent copies of the healing prayer and told the pastors to use it amongst the afflicted and oppressed.

The following powerful testimonies are from many of these pastors. They are written as I received them. Praise God for this healing prayer and the anointing upon it. I have only shared a small number of these testimonies.

....

"My name is Y Radha. I am thirty years old, married and with two children. My husband is working in Autonager as a marker. We have no house and are living in a rented home. I accepted Christ two years ago and my husband and I attend a Baptist Church that is near where we live. About fifty people come together to worship the Lord on a Sunday. In India about 80% of people are Hindu, 11% are Muslim and 8% are Christian. When the British were here, Christianity spread all over India. During those years seeds were sown and now people in all walks of life are converting to Christianity. All of my forefathers were Hindu and they worshipped creation and man made idols. Now the Light has come into our world.

I had been suffering with back pain for five years and had tried many kinds of pain killers but they were no use at all. Although I knew about healing, I had many doubts about it. For years I believed that medicines are given by God to help us. Because of this I did not really believe for healing. One day Pastor Dattu visited my home and prayed for my back pain, using the prayer letter which you sent him. God healed me completely and my faith has been greatly strengthened. Praise God.

....

Orphanage

Our churches look after fifteen children aged from eight to thirteen years, five girls and ten boys. God has done miracles for all our children. Recently a fever caused by a viral infection came into India from Africa. This was a new disease; doctors did not know how to treat it; there were no medicines; doctors were just prescribing paracetamol. For thirty three days all the children had been suffering with 104 degree fever, all over body pains and vomiting. They were unable to walk, unable to talk or eat any thing. I feared they were all going to die. In this critical situation and day of trouble your prayer letter with the healing scriptures arrived. I went to every child, touched them and prayed the healing prayer over them in Jesus name. God instantly healed every child. The fever left them completely. This miracle happened on 1ˢᵗ August 2006. Praise God.

Devesahayam
8/8/2006

....

I received this testimony from our local pastor M Premasamudram, Anandapuram village:

Date 2/11/2006

Mr K Tata Rao, aged thirty two is an employee of Coromandal Fertilisers Ltd. He is a welder in the plant and has a good salary. He lives in a nice house and lacks for nothing. He has a lot of money in the bank but wastes his money on bad habits. His life is like the prodigal son in the Bible in Luke 15. The Bible tells us the love of money is the

51

root of all evil. There are many people who are rich in the world's terms but they are not rich towards God. This is very sad. In Luke's gospel there are three rich fools on the highway to hell. We should use our riches to glorify God. People are eating, drinking, gambling, going with different women, eating in good hotels, wearing expensive clothes but these worldly pleasures can lead us into hell. Rich people never think about God. In the Bible there are many rich people. They are rich towards God. Having God in your life makes you truly rich. Money is very important in human life. Without money we can't do anything.

This man had relationships with many different women. Eventually AIDS entered his blood stream. Doctors tested his blood and the report was positive. He started to use very costly medicines. From day to day he lost his strength and could no longer enjoy relationships with women. Eventually he became so weak he was unable to walk and could not leave his bed. There was no hope for him. He was close to death. In this situation our pastor M Premasamudram visited his home and used your anointed prayer. Mr Rao confessed all the sins he had committed in his life and accepted Jesus as his Personal Saviour. His faith in Christ and your prayer healed him miraculously. Now he is well again and is a new creature. He has stopped all his bad habits and is serving the Lord. He is back at work and in his free time he is distributing tracts. In this way he is glorifying our Lord. Pray for him and his family.

M Premasamudram,
Anandapuram Village

....

Healed 7/01/2007
Name: M Papamma
Age   : 55 years
Disease: T.B

This lady, M Papamma is a Hindu and has been following this religion and its customs for many years. She prayed to many Hindu gods for healing but there was no reply. They are idols made by man. They have eyes but cannot see, ears but cannot hear, hands but cannot touch, legs but cannot walk, a mouth but cannot speak. These idols are not gods. M Papamma worshipped many idols and visited many large temples. She spent a lot of money trying to have her sins washed away. She lost all her family members and was totally alone. She had no peace, could not sleep, and was always coughing. She used many medicines and injections but it was all no use. She was like the woman in Mark 5:15 who had an issue of blood for twelve years and could find no help.

One day our pastor visited this lady and shared the gospel with her. He used your anointed prayer. God healed her from her TB. She accepted Jesus Christ as her Lord and is attending church. God touched her on 7/1/2007 at 10 am. God saved and healed her. Pray for this sister. Praise to God.

David (Pastor)

....

Healed 2/1/2007
Name: M Aswaradem
Age: 44 years
Disease: Stomach pains for 5 years

Our pastor visited this lady on 2/1/2007 and prayed for her stomach pain. She had been suffering from this pain for many years. Pastor David used your anointed prayer. God touched this lady and healed her instantly. Now she has no more pain. As a Hindu she had worshipped many Hindu gods, visited many temples, taken baths in holy rivers but nothing had helped. She had no peace. God healed her from her stomach pains and saved her on the same day. She confessed all her sins and accepted Christ as her Saviour and Lord. Now she is following Jesus Christ and attending church. Pray for this sister.

Pastor David

....

Healed 4/1/2007
Name: K Deevamma
Age: 50 years
Disease: Jaundice

This fifty year old lady called Deevamma was born into a Hindu family. She has two sons and three daughters who are all married and living away from home. These families depend on farming and they have animals such as cows, lambs, pigs, and buffalo. They cultivate rice fields and gardens where they grow coconut, mango and other fruit and vegetables to sell in the markets. Two years ago she was attacked by Jaundice. She tried English and Aryudic medicines but nothing helped. She turned yellow. Her body, fingers, nails, feet, eyes, even her urine turned yellow. She was close to death. Our pastor shared about the love of Christ and prayed for her. She is now well, totally healed. God visited her and spoke to her in the night. He raised her from death and saved her. Now she is attending church. Pray for her.

Pastor David

....

Healed: 8/1/2007
Name: N Sujata
Age: 60 years
Disease: Body pains

This sixty year old lady, N Sujata, had lost all her family members and was living in a bare hut with few possessions. She had once been a rich land lady but her husband had squandered all their money. She had lost her children and husband some years previously and was living by begging. Day by day she would call at homes and ask for food. She did not know anything about Jesus Christ as there was no church or pastor in her village. On 8/1/2007 at noon she was begging for food when our pastor met her and brought her to his home. He shared the gospel with her. She confessed her sins and accepted Christ. He washed away her sins with His blood. Then our pastor prayed for her body pains, using your anointed prayer. God healed her. Now she has no more pain. She saw the Lord Jesus in a vision. He talked with her and gave her eternal life.

Pastor David

....

One of our pastors, G Daniel, sent me the following testimony. In Kajuluru, one of our villages, there was a cruel man named M Rama Krushunudu. This man, aged 45 was a heavy drinker and associated with many women. He was a Hindu and hated the gospel of Jesus Christ, all Christians and pastors. He has beaten our pastor on many occasions. On Sundays he would throw stones at the thatched roof of our church and tried to trouble God's work in every way.

In August 2006 he had a serious accident when he fell under a lorry. They took him to the hospital but the doctors said he was dead. Our pastor visited him in hospital and used your anointed prayer. God heard our pastor's prayer and gave him life but his right leg was so badly damaged that the doctors wanted to remove it. Our pastor prayed for this leg and God healed it. Right there on the bed, this man confessed all his sins and bad deeds and accepted Christ as his Saviour. He embraced our pastor and asked his forgiveness. God healed him completely. This is a true and living testimony that happened in the village of Kajuluru. Now his leg is healed and he can walk again. He is serving the Lord and working with our pastor. God raised him from death, his leg was healed, and now he has the security of eternal life. God has performed a great miracle. Our pastor baptised him in water and changed his old Hindu name to M Israel. Please pray for him and for his family.

Y Devasahayam
19/10/2006

....

The following testimony was received from one of our pastors in Kajuluru village.

My name is R John Victor. I am a forty year old married man. My wife's name is Suseela, and she is thirty years old. We live in a thatched hut. I am a tailor and my wife also helps with the tailoring work. We both believe in the Lord Jesus and every Sunday we attend church and worship the Lord. We give tithes of what we earn every week. About sixty people attend our church. My pastor is a good man, a man of prayer and he can teach the Word of God. I also help the pastor with gospel meetings, tract distribution and in many other ways. Every day I read four chapters from the Bible, and we spend much time in prayer. Nothing is lacking in my home. God has blessed us with all things. Man needs food and clothing. We both love God with our whole hearts.

Every day is good for us as we are enjoying the Lord. We have received salvation and God is our Heavenly Father. Many years have passed and we have no children. We are both strong and healthy but God had closed my wife's womb. Last week our pastor visited my family with your anointed prayer. He opened the Bible and shared many things with us about Rachel, Sarah, Hanna and John the Baptist. This encouraged our faith. Our pastor kept assuring us that nothing is impossible with God. God wants to do good things for us. When we love God, He also loves us. The pastor shared many wonderful things from the Bible with us. He closed the message and asked us to kneel in prayer. He had the prayer you had sent him in his hand. He prayed and put the blessed prayer cloth on us. He also prayed over oil and blessed it, telling my wife to rub it on her stomach. God opened my

57

wife's womb and now she is pregnant. We both believed God is going to do miracles through your anointed prayer. Please pray for us, that God will give us children.

R John Victor
Uddandapuram

....

Healed 27/11/2006
Name: L Narayana
Age: 59 years

My name is L Narayana and I am 59 years old. As a Hindu I worshipped everything in the world – the sun, the moon, the stars, snakes, trees, cows, elephants, mother, father, and elderly people. All my life I followed human traditions but I was a hypocrite because there was no real spiritual life in me. I spent all my life in sinful ways and now I am an old woman. One day pastor visited me and told me the truth about Jesus Christ. For many years I had suffered pain all over my body and in my bones. I had used many pain killers but they did not take the pain away. When your pastor visited me and prayed over me using your anointed prayer cloth, God touched and healed me. His light came upon me. Now I have no pains at all. I am well. I have accepted Christ as my personal Saviour.

L Narayana

....

My name is B Jacob aged forty five. I was married at the age of twenty five and God gave me two children. I became ill and doctors told me I would die within months. I suffered paralysis after a stroke in the month of July. I had to use many medicines. Doctors told me I could not eat the following things- bananas, coconut milk, jack fruit, melon, beef, cheese, butter, milk, curds, pork, tomato, potato, new rice and many other common foods. I was told I should not walk in cool places and many other restrictions.

I could not walk, could not stand or go out to the latrine. I have faced a lot of suffering recently. I had to stop my tailoring work and because of this had no income and no food. Many people came to see me but no one could offer any help. I was alone. Even though I have a Biblical name,   Jacob, I knew nothing about Christ or salvation or healing. I never attended a church on Sunday. I had many bad habits and was spiritually dead and ready to go to hell.

In this situation Brother Y Devasahayam read your anointed prayer over me and rebuked the devil of paralysis in the name of Jesus. He prayed in a loud voice in the power of the Spirit and put your prayer letter on my head. I was shaken, all my body was shaken. God healed me. I confessed all my sins and invited Christ into my life. Now I am in Christ and Christ is in me. I am living for God and hope to be baptised soon. I can walk again. Doctors could not help me, medicines could not help me but God touched and healed me and has raised me up. Now I am living for His glory. Please pray for me and for my family. He touched me on 24/7/2006. Thank You Jesus, praise You, Jesus, lead me Jesus.

B Jacob

....

I received the following testimony from one of our village churches at Gantada Housing Colony on 15/8/2006.

Our pastor's name is P. Samuel. He told us what had happened. This lady called Eswaramma is thirty five years old. She has three children and lives in a thatched hut. She has some cows and provides for the family by selling their milk. Ten years ago she contracted TB and had to go to hospital, where she stayed for several months. When she was discharged, the hospital superintendent gave her some drugs and injections. She was told she must take these medicines without fail. She had no rest night or day because of her cough. She could not eat and was unable to sleep. She could not do any kind of work. She suffered with TB for ten years. She became very thin and weak.

Our local pastor read your anointed prayer letter over her. She knelt down on the floor and immediately light fell upon her. She fell down on the ground, praising Jesus and asking Him to forgive her sins. She invited Him to come into her heart.

Now she has no cough. She is eating, walking, talking with people, and having sound sleep. Day by day she is growing stronger. As a Hindu she worshipped many gods but since she has become a Christian she has stopped all idol worship. She has separated herself from her caste and people and has dedicated her life to Christ. On Sunday 20 August she was baptised by me in a water tank. Please pray for her and for her family salvation.

> P Samuel for Sister Eswaramma
> Gantada Housing Colony
> Visakhapatnam

....

I received the following testimony from our village pastor P Ratna Raju in Kannavanipalem Village.

> Name: S Appa Rao
> Age: 35 years
> Healed: 10/9/2006

Brother Appa Rao is a Hindu who has converted to Christianity and attends church every Sunday. He has two sons and a daughter. He and his wife keep ten buffalo and sell the milk in the village. He is a tall, thin man who damaged his back bone in an accident a few years ago. He spent a lot of money on hospitals and medicines. Doctors did their best for him but it was no use. He was unable to stand properly because his back bone was bent. His whole life changed. He could no longer do any thing for his family and felt useless.

I sent your anointed prayer to our pastor and explained how people were being healed through this. I also shared with him about your prison ministry. I sent your booklet "Nothing is impossible with God". I encouraged his faith to believe for healing. Our pastors know all the scriptures but do not apply them in a practical way. At Gospel Crusades people are told that Jesus Christ can heal you but this pastor had not experienced any healings. We need to have experience of healing so that we can help sick people around us.

Our pastor visited Appa Rao and used your anointed prayer with faith in his heart. He also anointed him with oil and prayed for his back bone problem. God touched him and power went into him. His body burned with the power of the Holy Spirit and your anointed prayer made him straight. This is a great miracle which God has done in our village. The whole church is praising God for this miracle. In the Bible, Jesus did many miracles and the same God is touching and healing people today. In this way people are coming to Christ and the church is growing in grace. Please pray for Brother Appa Rao and his family.

....

Date: 14/8/2006

Dear Martin Tuson and family,

Greetings to you from our Indian Churches, pastors and orphans. We are all well and pray for you and for your ministry every day. God has done great miracles through the healing prayer which God gave you many years ago. In my church there are eight asthmatics who have suffered for many years and have to use medicines on a daily basis. This is costing them a lot of money in doctor's fees. After I received your healing prayer I called all these asthmatics together and conducted a healing meeting. I read your healing prayer over each one of them. Now weeks have passed and there is no more asthma. All are well. We are glad to inform you about *this great miracle. All eight former Hindus have now been baptised by me in water. They have been coming to the church for many years but were not baptised. After the healing they repented of their sins, cried out to God for forgiveness and invited Christ into their hearts. They have given up their Hindu customs, stopped all idol worship and are growing in grace. Please pray for these new converts.*

....

Chapter 12

Delivered from Epilepsy

"Jesus went forth and saw a great multitude and was moved
with compassion toward them and He healed their sick"
(Matthew 14:14)

Yes, Christ Jesus had compassion for individuals as well as for the multitudes. He has given me this same compassion for the lost and the sick. I thank Him that I have been a witness to His grace and mercy.

I remember taking a meeting in a small chapel in Devon (Langtree). It was a Methodist congregation and they desperately needed to witness the power of God. There was a lady sitting at the back who had a long list of health problems. As I mingled with the congregation I stopped with her and asked her what it was she wanted God to do for her. She explained that she had suffered a stroke and as a result of that she was suffering paralysis on the right side of her body. She had no feeling in her hand or arm.

I remember that when I placed my hand on her shoulder and started to pray, I felt her collar bone moving back and forth. It was a strange sensation. When I finished praying she shouted," What did you do to me? What did you do to me?" I assured her that I had not done anything but that God's power had gone into her body. All feeling came back to her paralysed side. She was amazed. Another elderly gentleman had his hearing restored. He took out his hearing aid and was able to hear perfectly. God worked many miracles over the five days I was there. It was also a privilege to minister in Dartmoor Prison where we saw three men saved and five restored in their relationship with the Lord.

You are probably wondering what this chapter has to do with epilepsy. I will let Brother Oliver Moone share his testimony. This miracle took place in Lusaka Central Prison, Zambia.

"Before being brought to prison I had never suffered from epilepsy but while serving my sentence I contracted this terrible disease and it has troubled me for some time. The doctor prescribed phenobarbitone but it did not change anything. My attacks became so severe that sometimes I fell and hurt myself badly.

When news of a group of Christian inmates who were praying for healing reached me, I decided to invite them to come and pray for me. They prayed and asked me to open my heart and ask God to deliver me. They finished and it seemed as if nothing at all had happened.

It was only after a week that I came to realize I was no longer having attacks. I couldn't believe this and thought that maybe the demon was giving me a grace period, but the epilepsy never came back. As I am writing this testimony I have clocked two months without any attacks and most of my friends can't believe that the Lord has healed me. I thank Jesus for this and I will never stop loving Him. He really is a merciful God. "Ask and it shall be given you". Help was truly given to me at the right time. Amen."

....

Chapter 13

Hugh's Testimony

"For we cannot but speak the things which we have seen
and heard"
(Acts 4:20)

This is a wonderful testimony and I have shared it with many people. It has even been made into a tract. Hugh also shared about this miracle on revelation TV. God has been glorified through all of this. I will let Hugh share what took place that Sunday when he encountered the power of the Risen Saviour. This is now a case study in the Royal Victoria Hospital in Belfast.

"My name is Hugh Wilson. I was born in Belfast in 1960 and brought up on the peace line between the Shankill and the Falls Road. I gave my life to Christ when I was 16 years of

age. I am married to Lynne and we have three daughters. We eventually came to live in Bangor.

I had worked in the Post Office for about eighteen years, when I decided to have a change of career and took a job in sales which I really enjoyed. After a short period of unemployment, the first time in my life that I had been without work, I quickly found a job doing deliveries. I was only a few weeks in this job when I started to experience pain in my right shoulder. Two years previously I had fallen in the Post Office and had damaged my shoulder. I don't think it ever healed correctly.

I was taken to the Royal Victoria Hospital where they examined my shoulder and found it to be inflamed and swollen. They gave me some pain killers and tablets to reduce the swelling. Then a couple of days later when I was getting dressed, my shoulder locked completely. To be honest, I had never experienced pain like it before. I didn't know what to do, because my arm was powerless and I could not lift anything at all. I was rushed back up to the hospital. The doctors told me that the muscle had come away from the bone and that the bone had calcified and locked, resulting in a bad dislocation. They pointed out that this was an unusual case and would take a long time to put right.

This left me in a real predicament as I had just started a new job, but whatever troubles I face in life, my first port of call is God. I prayed that something good would come out of this. I phoned my employer, told him the problem and continued to receive injections for the pain. Although I could only manage restricted movement of thirty degrees with my arm, I returned to work struggling to complete my daily tasks using only my good arm.

One Sunday morning I came into church and Martin asked me if he could pray for me after the service. I had mixed emotions about everything at this stage and, to my shame, even tried to avoid Martin after the service. He collared me as he always does and we went into one of the classrooms where he prayed the simplest prayer. Halfway through the prayer he said to me, "Hugh, that lump has gone." When he had finished praying, he asked me to lift my arm above my head, an action which would have been an impossible task when I only had thirty degrees of movement! I lifted it above my head, around my back, and anywhere I wanted to. I was completely amazed! I know I shouldn't have been so startled, for I know that God still heals today! God completely healed that injury in an instant. Praise Him! I believe that the Lord was saying to me; "I love you and I am still here with you, even through the hard times."

The hospital still wanted me to attend physiotherapy, which I did. I received a phone call from one of the orthopaedic consultants at the Royal Victoria Hospital and I called to see him. He was completely amazed when I moved my arm and shoulder quite freely without pain. "What happened to you?" he asked. I replied, "God has healed me!" I went on to tell him how I had been prayed for in church and how God had touched me. He said, "Oh, our injections must have helped, but it takes a couple of weeks for these things to sort themselves out." I told him that the healing occurred only two days after the injection had been given. "God has healed me; it's as simple as that." I explained to him how I had been in agony *and how limited my movement had been until I was prayed for, when in an instant I was healed. He said; "Can I take another x-ray?" Another x-ray was taken with startling results. It appeared that it was the shoulder of someone else, because there was no damage there at all, whereas the original x-ray had revealed extensive injuries. The consultant told me that I was a most unusual case.*

I know that God touched me at a time in my life when I needed it most. I thank and praise Him and pray that whoever reads this will come to know that He is very real. The greatest miracle of all is when a man or woman puts their faith and trust in Christ. God loves you and has a plan and purpose for your life. I pray that through this simple tract you will come to know Christ in your own life.

....

Chapter 14

Being Bold

"Now when they saw the boldness of Peter and John and perceived that they were unlearned and ignorant men, they marvelled: and they took knowledge of them that they had been with Jesus" (Acts 4:13)

With boldness, miracles will always follow, as I shared at the beginning of this book. Many times we feel led by the Spirit to pray for someone or to do something for the Lord. Yes, then fear enters, fear of the unknown, fear that nothing will happen. "For God has not given us the spirit of fear, but of power and of love and of a sound mind." (2 Timothy 1:17)

Make that part of your prayer life that God would impart boldness upon you. As I walk the wings in HM Prison Maghaberry I need boldness. Many times when I

71

have been praying for inmates, I will tell them that I believe God's power will touch them there and then. Praise God it does happen, leaving them in no doubt of God's sovereign power and love towards them.

One question I am always asked is about how I feel when someone I pray for is not healed. To be honest, in the early days this would always play on my mind. But now, after praying with so many people, I have come to understand it is God Who is sovereign: He is the One Who heals. There have been times when I have prayed with someone for a particular area of healing, and the Lord has touched them in a different way to what I asked.

I have also had experiences where I have sensed 100% that a miracle is going to take place. You have read many wonderful testimonies about healing through the anointed healing prayer that God has given me. When the Lord gave me that prayer many years ago, He told me to send it out to those who were sick. For the past five years I have done just that. When I first started to send the healing prayer out within the prisons, I did not receive any word back or any testimonies for about eight months.

Throughout that eight month period I continued to send it out. Why? I was being obedient to the Holy Spirit. Can you just imagine for one minute what would have happened if I had not been obedient? The healing of many bodies and saving of many souls would not have happened. It is always good to obey the voice of God. There have been thousands of healing miracles through this prayer. When the Lord does something there are no half measures. What has God been speaking into your heart? Be encouraged. God wants to use you in a mighty way. Just think, when you get to glory, you will have a knock on your mansion door. You will open the door and there will be the Apostle Paul standing and he will say:

"I have heard so many things about you; I just had to meet you and shake your hand." Praise God!

We serve a miracle working God. Truly, nothing is impossible to Him; you don't have to hang in there with God; He has your hand and He won't let go. As Christians we sometimes look at individuals in the Ministry and think it's alright for them. Do you think the disciples were well educated men? In those days fishermen were regarded as the lowest of the low. I'm sure some of them struggled with reading and writing. Look how God was able to use them for His Glory. This can be you too.

My own Christian walk began when I was saved on 7th November 1982. For almost half of my Christian life I was "doing the religious thing", just going through the motions. I thought God could never use the likes of me. I know I am talking to some of you now as you are reading this chapter. It's hitting home with you. You are thinking that you have no gifts and wondering what you could possibly do. Believe me, I have been there.

You ask, "Martin, what does it take?" My answer is:" complete surrender and submission to the King of Kings." If you have to get on your face then do so. Study His word; it's really powerful. Spend time in His presence. For me it means complete surrender, every single day. Yes it can be tough, but so what? With the Lord on our side, we have no worries. Please my friends; be encouraged. I feel the Holy Spirit has written this chapter as my pen would not stop.

I remember one Friday afternoon in Maghaberry Prison I believed so strongly for God to perform a miracle. I prayed for an inmate with a serious shoulder injury. Straight after the prayer I asked him how he felt. He said he felt just the same; nothing had happened. Now right there and then I could have just said, "Well, God bless" and made a hasty exit. But I was so convinced that I asked him again a few minutes later. Guess what? He said he felt the pain shifting. Two minutes later he was completely healed. Now that took the Lord's boldness.

I want to end this chapter with a testimony of healing. Listen to how Ester was bold in praying for her son, even when at first nothing happened.

....

Dear Martin,

Sometime ago my little boy, aged nine, dislocated his shoulder. I was alone in the house at the time. The pain was so intense that he became faint. I treated him the best I knew how but kept holding the thought that as soon as someone came, I would run for help. He seemed to get worse and cried very much. I undressed him and tried to twist his arm into place, but it caused him so much suffering that I began to get afraid. Then like a flash came a thought and with that a sense of calm and trust. I lost all fear. I asked the child if I could read him the healing prayer. He said "Yes Mamma." I began reading it aloud to him. After about half an hour he tried to lift his arm but screamed and again became very pale. I continued to read aloud and again he made an effort to put some candy into his mouth. This time I noticed, with joy, that he almost reached his mouth before he felt the pain. I kept reading aloud to him until my sister and my two boys came in. Suddenly he jumped off his bed because he was so delighted to see his brothers. He forgot all about his arm. He then began to tell his aunt that he had broken his arm but mamma had treated it with the healing prayer. He was playing out doors as if nothing had happened.

Mrs Ester Davies Mulenga
Ibex Hill
Lusaka
Zambia

....

Chapter 15

Phone Ministry

"But be ye doers of the Word and not hearers only,
deceiving your own selves."
(James 1:22)

I thank the true and living God for the miracles which have been manifested as I have prayed over the phone for individuals. You will already have read some of these testimonies in earlier chapters of this book. Even today I received an e-mail from Pakistan. My brother in Christ, Amir, phoned me a few weeks back to say that his brother was very ill. So right there and then I prayed for him. At the very time I was praying for him, God's power came upon him as he lay in his sick bed. He woke the next morning completely healed by our Risen Saviour. He was not aware at the time that we were praying for him. Praise God for His power.

I remember on another occasion praying for an elderly lady who was house bound. She could not walk without the use of a Zimmer frame. She was in great pain. As I prayed for God's power to touch her, she started to cry. All of the pain left her body. I told her to walk without the use of her Zimmer frame. She walked as if it had never been a problem. I think she ended up running around the house singing God's praises.

I was over in London appearing on a Christian TV station. I was staying in a friend's flat. When I was there he received a phone call from a lady who needed healing. He handed the phone to me. Her name was Mia and she was riddled with arthritis. She had been in pain for many years and her movement was limited. After I prayed for Mia she said she felt a strange sensation going up her arms and throughout her body. She was healed instantly and was singing God's praises. She asked me to pray for her daughter Cathy, who was suffering from Fibromialga. So I prayed for Cathy that the Lord would touch and heal her and that this would be another testimony.

Praise God she too was healed. All of the pain that was in her hands and feet left her. About four hours later I appeared on the show. Halfway through the phone lines were opened and guess who phoned in? Mia! She testified to both her own and her daughter's healing. She said that they were both doing things that they could not do before without being in pain. It was a powerful testimony to our Risen Saviour that night.

One elderly lady I prayed for over the phone was suffering from the damage caused by a stroke. Her hand was in the shape of a claw and there was no movement in it. After I prayed with her, she put the phone down and noticed her hand drop to her side and all of her fingers opened up. Praise God for another wonderful miracle. Let that be an encouragement to you. Many of us may not be able to physically go and pray with a person, but it is so easy to pick up a phone and pray. I have prayed for people from as far away as Jamaica and America. Many miracles have also taken place as inmates have called me and I have prayed and seen God heal them. I could share so many more testimonies of folks who have been healed over the phone. Again, what a mighty and awesome God we serve. I have even seen the Lord touch and heal sceptics over the phone. Maybe there is someone reading this book today and this is a ministry the Lord wants you to have.

One thing I have noticed, when you pray for someone either personally or over the phone, is that people are touched that you take time for them. We know the Lord took time for people and would never turn anyone away. So praise God for the phone ministry. Maybe there is someone you know just waiting for a call?

....

Chapter 16

Only Believe

"As soon as Jesus heard the word that was spoken, He said to the ruler of the synagogue 'Be not afraid, only believe' ".
(Mark 5:36)

When you look up the word "believe" in the dictionary, you will read the words:-"to trust, to have faith". It is a word that should be very much evident in a Christian's life today. When you think about it, if you were to witness God perform an amazing miracle, that's all it would take for you to keep on praying for individuals, even if it did not happen again. Why? Because you have witnessed that God can do it and that's enough in itself. I remember the very first miracle I witnessed about five years ago. I prayed for an inmate at Maghaberry prison. I didn't even ask him how he felt afterwards. I just said "God Bless. See you next week." A few days later I got a letter from him telling me that God had healed him. Now once I have prayed for someone, I immediately ask them how they feel.

The following two testimonies from Peter and T.T Loops again show the power and anointing that is within the healing prayer. I have also included the healing prayer after these testimonies.

....

23 January 2005

Dear Martin,

I was healed of very bad rheumatism simply by reading the healing prayer. I had tried many medicines and massage but with no result. Doctors told me that I would always suffer from the disease as it was inherited and also because I had had rheumatic fever as a child. I suffered day and night and nothing could bring relief. But the healing prayer showed that I was wrong in believing nothing could help me. I gave up all the medicines I was taking and I have not touched any since then. That is over ten months ago. Before that I had often tried to do without a medicine that I had taken every day for five years, but I was always ill and had to return to it. Then I found the Only Medicine that helped and now I am freed from my suffering.

Peter Smith
Lukanga Delkins
Kabwe
Zambia

....

15 September 2005

Dear Martin,

I was in the midst of trouble facing cancer and all its uncertainties. Would the surgery be successful? Would the cancer come back? How would my family cope if I were to die? I woke up with such thoughts every morning and climbed into bed with them every night. The dark cloud of cancer surrounded me even though I tried to listen to the promises of God. When I read Zophar's words in Job 11:16, it seemed impossible that my trouble would ever recede into the background "like waters gone by". But I stood on tip toe in faith reaching out timidly and asking God to make this improbable promise true for me.

Months later, I rediscovered this copy of your healing prayer. As I read the words aloud, my spirit echoed back "Yes! It's true!" With surprise and joy I recognised that cancer no longer dominated my thoughts and daily activities. I could live my life free from its grip. Of course, having cancer changed me in many ways, mostly for good, but I was amazed to see that my trouble had flowed past, receding into a memory. The Lord had made this verse, once beyond my grasp, now part of my everyday reality.

TT Loops
Ritwe
Zambia

....

The Healing Prayer

Lord, I come before you now with a thankful heart. Precious Saviour, You have spoken to me about Your healing power. Many, Lord, are suffering in their physical bodies. Lord, I write this letter now and pray for those who read it to know Your healing power upon their afflicted bodies.

Lord, I take authority over every disease and sickness which is afflicting my brothers and sisters. I claim this authority with the authority you have given me as your disciple.

PSALM 103:3
"WHO FORGIVETH ALL THINE INIQUITIES AND HEALETH ALL THY DISEASES."

Lord, I pray for your power to be demonstrated today by stretching forth Your healing hand and that Your healing power and virtue will flow into bodies that are afflicted.

JOHN 14: 12-14
"VERILY, VERILY I SAY UNTO YOU: HE THAT BELIEVETH ON ME, THE WORKS THAT I DO, SHALL HE DO ALSO, AND GREATER WORKS THAN THESE SHALL HE DO, BECAUSE I GO TO MY FATHER. AND WHATSOEVER YOU ASK IN MY NAME, THAT WILL I DO, THAT THE FATHER MAY BE GLORIFIED IN THE SON. IF YOU ASK ANYTHING IN MY NAME I WILL DO IT."

In the name of Jesus Christ and with faith in that name, I pray for healing. Lord, I speak out against this problem in the flesh.

ACTS 4:30
"BY STRETCHING FORTH THINE HAND TO HEAL, AND THAT SIGNS AND WONDERS MAY BE DONE BY THE NAME OF THY HOLY CHILD, JESUS."

Lord, I thank You that You have heard this prayer and I praise You that you will bring healing through Your word, for we claim this in Jesus name. Today, Lord, Your name will be glorified in this place and this will be a testimony to Your power. Thank You, Lord for your grace and mercy. We give You all the honour, for You alone are worthy.

....

Chapter 17

The name of Jesus

"God also bearing witness, both with signs and wonders and
with divers miracles and gifts of the Holy Ghost, according to
His own will"
(Hebrews 2:4)

In the book of Philippians, Chapter 2, verse 10, it says
that …"at the name of Jesus every knee shall bow, of things
in heaven and things on earth and things under the earth."
That pretty much covers everything, for when I pray for
an individual, I am not coming in my own name or in any
authority which I have. I come in the name of the Lord
Jesus Christ, the Son of the Living and True God and in
His Kingdom authority. Oh, how wonderful is that name;
the very demons quake at that name!

The following testimonies of healing again show the
compassion of Christ for those within the prison cell.

....

16 October 2005

Brother Martin,

I am writing to you because an inmate here handed me your address and told me about how your printed prayers had healed another prisoner here. He told me that you are the first real Christian he had ever met in his whole life. To me it was just a story yet something within me urged me to accept this address. When I stretched out my hand to take the address, he told me not to forget him if God blessed me through this man.

Michael's state of health was a total mess due to an unknown sickness. The doctors needed money before they would treat him, and he could not even feel sure it would help. I felt the only thing I could do for him was to help in sourcing the money. I came to your office with this problem expecting financial assistance from you, but what you gave me was just what my friend needed most. God knows how to handle His people. When I told Michael you had sent him a healing booklet instead of money, his comments were not encouraging. Three days later, after another financial disappointment, he asked for the booklet.

After reading the booklet he quoted Philippians 2:10, 11(see above), and started telling us about Acts 3:6, 7

"Then Peter said, Silver and gold have I none: but such as I have give I thee: in the name of Jesus Christ of Nazareth rise up and walk. And he took him by the right hand and lifted him up and immediately his feet and bones received strength."

He also referred to John 14:12
"He that believeth on me, the works that I do shall he do also; and greater works than these shall he do, because I go unto my Father"

After referring to all these scriptures he prayed and then threw his bags of medication into the waste paper basket. That very day the Lord healed his son, our pastor and child of God whom Satan, the Master of Lies, wanted to destroy through this affliction.

Michael himself will write to you. Through this miracle others are now attending our church. When he gave his testimony there were shouts of "Praise the Lord."

....

Before I was brought into prison I was a Christian but with little faith. Sometimes I didn't even go to church and instead would go somewhere to drink beer. When I was locked up in a cell I felt as if I had been thrown into a deep ditch. I felt that I was sinking into depression and loneliness.

I called out to God from these prison walls from the depth of my heart and He heard me. I made a fresh start but I knew I had to change my way of thinking. In my despair a voice whispered to me that I was never alone. Although I was *locked up, in Christ I was free. From that time I dedicated my life to God. I heard the phrase about being free in prison but a prisoner outside of prison.*

Whilst in prison, I joined the football referee team and officiated at prison games. After abut a year I started feeling pain deep within the bones of my legs. I tried to take medicine from the prison clinic but it did not help. Then I met Brother Kalinchingabesa and he prayed for me on two occasions. Praise God, my problem is gone. God is great. Now I am able to run on the football pitch and do any physical exercise.

Samuel Mulinga
Maximum Security Prison
Zambia

....

25.08.06
Dear Brother Martin,

Grace to you and peace from God our Father and our Lord Jesus Christ who has blessed us with every spiritual blessing of healing power in the heavenly places in Christ, just as He chose us in Him before the foundation of the world, that we should be without blame before Him in love. Martin, God has predestined us to adoption as sons by Jesus Christ to Himself, according to the good pleasure of His will to the praise of the glory of His grace, by which He made us accepted in the beloved. I thank God for the help and compassion He has shown in my life and that through the healing prayer He has made me well.

Brother, the healing cards you sent are having effect on the inmates in the prison here. I went through to eight sick prisoners in different cells, many of them suffering from malaria, chest pains and other chronic illnesses. We sat with them and sang a song of praise and then went into a worship chorus. During this time I saw them crying, beating on their chests and asking the Son of God to forgive them. After a few minutes I encouraged them from the scriptures. I read Romans 10:9

"If you confess with your mouth the Lord Jesus and believe in your heart that God raised Him from the dead, you will be saved."

I also read from your card Psalm 103:3
"Who forgives all our sins and heals all our diseases."

I explained to them how God had healed me from my spinal cord problem. They were all convicted and straight away I led them into the prayer of repentance. They accepted Jesus as their personal Saviour and said that this time they would continue believing God.

After we had talked further about the salvation that is in Christ Jesus, I used your prayer card and asked them to pray with me, with thanks giving. After I had finished praying, each one of them seemed to fall into a light sleep. After a few minutes I asked them how they felt and they said that their pains and fever had completely gone.

Brother Martin, seeing eight of my fellow inmates healed has greatly encouraged my faith in God. I praise the Mighty God for what He is doing in this place. Through this healing these prisoners have come to know the true God. They now understand that through Jesus Christ there is no condemnation to them. I hope to continue with this ministry outside of the prison and I long to see God's healing power extended in hospitals and in orphanages where people like me spent our childhoods. I will leave my prayer card in my pocket because it is my defense. Just as God has chosen you to have this grace gift, so too I long for it to be part of my life. I want to see people touched with the love of God and to be a blessing to others as you have been to me.

I would like to request postage and writing materials so that these men can write to you themselves.

May the Lord bless you.

Yours in Christ
James Mwanse

Chapter 18

To God be the Glory

"That your faith should not stand in the wisdom of men, but in the power of God."
(I Corinthians 2:5)

I pray that you will have been blessed by this book and that God, through the power of the Holy Spirit, will have spoken into your life. If you are not a born again Christian, my prayer is that you will accept Christ into your own life. You will see from what you have just read that God loves you and He wants to use you. Yes, He has a destiny for you to fulfil.

If you want to make that decision today, just pray this simple prayer:

"Lord, I realize that I am a sinner and that I need to be forgiven. I believe that You are the Son of God and that You died for me. Forgive me for the sins that I have committed. Come into my heart and life from this very day. Fill me with your Holy Spirit and, by Your grace, I will follow You for the rest of my life. Amen."

Please feel free to contact me. The details are at the start of this book. I want to thank my Heavenly Father for every testimony in this book. He alone receives all the glory, honour and praise.

"Thank you, Lord"

Printed in the United Kingdom
by Lightning Source UK Ltd.
126012UK00001B/46-138/A